CENTRAL LONDON THEN & NOW

IN COLOUR

LAINA WATT

The History Press

This book is dedicated to the marvellous friends

I found in London – most of all,

Anne, Carolyn and Christina

First published in 2012

The History Press
The Mill, Brimscombe Port
Stroud, Gloucestershire, GL5 2QG
www.thehistorypress.co.uk

© Laina Watt, 2012

The right of Laina Watt to be identified as the Author
of this work has been asserted in accordance with the
Copyrights, Designs and Patents Act 1988.

British Library Cataloguing in Publication Data.
A catalogue record for this book is available from the British Library.

ISBN 978 0 7524 6552 4

Typesetting and origination by The History Press
Manufacturing managed by Jellyfish Print Solutions Ltd
Printed in India.

CONTENTS

ABOUT THE AUTHOR

Laina Watt is an author and professional photographer living in South East England and working worldwide. Since her graduation from Central St Martin's College of Art, her photographs have been showcased in the press, and exhibited in locations both in the UK and Europe. Her contemporary approach to architectural photography has gained her a reputation for delivering distinctive and highly imaginative photographs of London. She is particularly interested in the juxtaposition of old and new in a constantly evolving cityscape, and this forms a recurring theme in her photography.

Laina's photographs are available to buy as prints and canvases online at www.photos-of-london.com.

INTRODUCTION

London's streets are a fascinating juxtaposition of old and new, with Roman stones and Saxon churches, Norman fortresses, Tudor palaces and Victorian bridges jostling for space with the futuristic glass and steel creations of contemporary architects. London's distinctive skyline has evolved organically over the centuries into a quintessentially British silhouette. The elegant dome of Sir Christopher Wren's famed cathedral, Sir Norman Foster's quirky Gherkin-shaped office building and Sir Giles Gilbert Scott's Bankside Power Station (since transformed into the Tate Modern) each speak of different eras in London's history and yet coexist happily.

Many of the atmospheric sepia photographs featured in this book date to the 1890s, when the art of photography was still a novelty and London's thoroughfares were still the realm of horse-drawn carts, glimmering gas lamps, 'pea-souper' fogs and Oliver Twist-style urchins. One can easily imagine Sherlock Holmes striding purposefully down one of these streets with his top hat and cane, on the trail of villains.

Seeking out the same viewpoint from which to create contemporary photographs was an interesting though not always easy task. In some cases the scene had changed so much as to be unrecognisable, in many cases due to the German bombing raids of the Blitz. Also, in contrast to these romantic old images, today it is a challenge to photograph modern London without featuring the ever-present fast-food outlets, chain stores, CCTV cameras, parked cars and executives talking into mobile phones. However, in some cases the scenes remain remarkably unchanged, showing pockets of London which have altered little in over 100 years.

London's lively history is written into the fabric of its streets, and anyone who takes the time to look around and explore will be well rewarded. One could fill this book several times over with interesting scenes and landmarks found in central London, and in compiling the photographs for this book I have discovered many hidden gems that I never knew existed, despite having lived in the city for several years.

LONDON EYE AND
THE GREAT WHEEL
AT EARLS COURT

THE GREAT WHEEL was built for the Empire of India exhibition of 1895 at Earls Court in west London. At 94m (300ft) it was, at the time, the largest wheel of its kind in the world. Modelled on the original Ferris wheel in Chicago, this gigantic wheel afforded visitors extensive aerial views over the city, reaching as far as Windsor Castle on a clear day. The wheel was an impressive feat of engineering, taking over a year to construct. It weighed over 1,100 tons and was powered by 100hp steam engines and chain gears, taking twenty minutes to complete each revolution. It was a hugely popular attraction for both Londoners and tourists, despite the fact that in May 1896 the wheel got stuck, leaving passengers stranded for four-and-a-half hours.

THIS ATTRACTION WAS dismantled in 1907, but today it has been reincarnated in the form of the London Eye on the South Bank of the river Thames. Designed by the husband-and-wife team of architects Julia Barnfield and David Marks, it quickly became one of London's most iconic and best-loved landmarks. Visited by over 3.5 million people annually since its opening in January 2000, the Eye is the most popular attraction in the UK. At 135m, the London Eye is the tallest such wheel in Europe and, like the Great Wheel, is an impressive work of contemporary engineering. Its construction required 1,700 tons of steel and forty-four concrete supports sunk 33m deep into 2,200 tons of concrete to safely support this massive structure. There are many other striking similarities between the old Earls Court Wheel and today's London Eye. Both wheels share a basic spoked structure, a lot like a bicycle wheel. However, the wooden carriages of the Great Wheel have been replaced with thirty-two space-age, pod-like glass capsules – one to represent each borough of London – which allow unobstructed 360° views of the city. Each revolution takes half an hour, and, as the Eye travels slowly, passengers can walk on and off without the wheel stopping. The location of the London Eye is far superior to the Great Wheel, positioned on the river close to Big Ben and the Houses of Parliament, and affords unbeatable views of the city's stunning architecture.

Like its Victorian counterpart, the London Eye is designed to have the simple function of allowing people to 'fly' above the capital and view it from above. Architect Sir Richard Rogers says: 'The Eye has done for London what the Eiffel Tower did for Paris, which is to give it a symbol and to let people climb above the city and look back down on it. Not just specialists or rich people, but everybody. That's the beauty of it: it is public and accessible, and it is in a great position at the heart of London.' (Marks Barfield Architects, *Eye: The Story Behind the London Eye*, Black Dog Publishing, London, 2007)

WESTMINSTER BRIDGE

THE ELEGANT, GOTHIC arches of Westminster Bridge span the river Thames between the boroughs of Lambeth and Westminster. For centuries the only bridge across the river was the ancient London Bridge to the east. Lambeth Horse-ferry was the only means of crossing the Thames at this point, and this remained the case until 1736 when plans were passed by Parliament for the construction of a new bridge at Westminster. This stone bridge was completed in 1750 – though a century later it was subsiding badly and in need of replacing. The current bridge was designed by British engineer Thomas Page and opened on 24 May 1862. The seven-arch wrought-iron bridge has an overall length of 252m (826.8ft) and a span of 26m (88ft), with Gothic detailing by Charles Barry, architect of the nearby Palace of Westminster. It is the oldest bridge in central London.

Thanks to the bridge's prime location linking some of London's best-loved landmarks – City Hall and the London Eye on the southern bank, and Big Ben and the Houses of Parliament on the northern bank – Westminster Bridge has been immortalised in many films and television programmes, including *28 Days Later*, *Monty Python's Flying Circus* and *Doctor Who*. In the past, it has also inspired paintings by artists such as J.M.W. Turner and Canaletto, and the sonnet 'Composed upon Westminster Bridge', describing the view of London early in the morning, by the poet William Wordsworth.

The charming old stereograph opposite dates from 1901 and shows the scene as it would have appeared over a century ago. The bridge is busy with traffic in the form of horse-drawn taxis and a wagon laden with crates. A man pulls a handcart towards Westminster and a street sweeper cleans the road. Smartly dressed gentlemen wearing top hats and ladies in sombre-looking Victorian dresses and shawls go on their way. In the background stand Big Ben and the Houses

of Parliament. Westminster Bridge was the first roadway in the city to have street lighting, and ornate gas lamps line the bridge. These would originally have been lit by lamplighters at dusk every evening.

TODAY, WESTMINSTER BRIDGE with its prime location still offers fantastic views along the river. As a result it is often crowded with tourists and photographers, along with the usual London commuters. This contemporary photograph was taken at dusk from a vantage point slightly upriver, affording a view of the whole bridge with the floodlit Palace of Westminster in the background. Between 2005 and 2007 the bridge underwent a complete refurbishment, including replacing the iron fascias and repainting the whole bridge in a distinctive turquoise colour. Despite this, the bridge looks virtually identical to how it did a century ago, though today the gas lamps have been replaced by electric street lamps. (Old image courtesy of the Library of Congress, LC-DIG-ppmsca-06808)

THE HOUSES OF PARLIAMENT

THE HOUSES OF PARLIAMENT at Westminster are among the world's most iconic buildings. Located to the west of the city, overlooking the Thames, this site has played a key role in England's history for nearly 1,000 years. Westminster became home to the kings of England from the eleventh century until 1512, when the palace was destroyed by fire. Thereafter the palace was replaced with more modest buildings and became the seat of England's parliament until this also burnt down. The new Houses of Parliament, which are so familiar to us today,

were built in lavish Gothic style by architect Sir Charles Barry. His young assistant, Augustus Pugin, designed the equally ornate interior. Work on the building began in 1840 and took thirty years to complete. Barry's design ingeniously incorporated surviving parts of the old royal palace, including Westminster Hall, the Jewel Tower, crypt and chapel.

This beautiful sepia photograph was taken from the Albert Embankment on the opposite side of the Thames, which offers perhaps the best view of this magnificent building. From this angle you get an idea of the huge scale of the Palace of Westminster, which covers 8 acres along with a further 4 acres of gardens. The Victoria Tower (named after Queen Victoria) can be seen on the left-hand side. At nearly 100m (325ft) high, this ornate tower was designed as the royal entrance to the building and also to house the parliamentary archives. The famous clock tower that houses the bell Big Ben can be seen to the right.

IN THIS MODERN photograph the palace is viewed from directly across the river, giving a sense of scale of the palace's impressive 300m-long façade. Taken at dusk on a summer's evening, the building is spectacularly floodlit, the lights reflected by the river. Despite being hit by fourteen German bombs during the Blitz, this beautiful building looks as good as new. Today the Houses of Parliament are a Grade I listed building, and a UNESCO World Heritage site.

THE EMBANKMENT

THE SWEEP OF the Victoria Embankment reaches for over a mile along the river from Blackfriars Bridge to Westminster. A major feat of nineteenth-century engineering was required to transform this previously unusable stretch of marshy land bordering the Thames into the 100ft-wide tree-lined promenade seen today. The idea of building the Embankment was originally conceived by Sir Christopher Wren, but it wasn't until 200 years later that Victorian engineering allowed this ambitious project to come to fruition. It was overseen by renowned civil engineer and city planner Sir Joseph Bazalgette. Quite aside from providing a

romantic location for Victorians seeking a riverside stroll in the handsome public gardens, the Embankment was created to house one of the city's main sewers, and also to relieve traffic congestion on Fleet Street and The Strand. During the ten years it took to construct, an impressive 37 acres of ground were reclaimed from the river. In this view taken from Waterloo Bridge around 1894, a crowded steamboat heads downstream on a cloudless, sunny day while gentlemen saunter along the promenade.

TODAY'S EMBANKMENT HAS itself changed little since its completion in 1870 and still provides a shady oasis in contrast to the bustling Strand to which it runs parallel. However, many of the buildings along this stretch of the Embankment were destroyed during the Blitz, and have since been replaced by modern office buildings. In this eastward view taken from Waterloo Bridge, the dome of St Paul's Cathedral remains unchanged, though it now competes for its place on London's horizon with the Gherkin, Tower 42 and the other modern skyscrapers of London's Square Mile. At the far right of the modern photograph, near to Blackfriars Bridge, the First World War ship HMS *President* can be seen in its mooring of eighty years. The ship is now a floating bar and venue.

NIGHT VIEW OF
THE RIVER THAMES

THIS ATMOSPHERIC OLD stereograph shows the view upriver from Waterloo Bridge.
At 11 p.m., when this picture was taken, gas lamps glimmer along the length of the Victoria
Embankment, and the river Thames gleams in the bright moonlight. The Embankment was
finished shortly before this picture was taken and the new trees are little more than saplings. The

distinctive silhouette of Big Ben's clock tower and the Houses of Parliament can be seen in the distance. On the opposite side of the river from Parliament, the outline of St Thomas's Hospital, with its distinctive turrets, can be made out. Taken before the era of electric lighting, the landmarks in this picture are not floodlit as they are at this time of night today and, indeed, only the clock face of Big Ben's clock tower is illuminated. However, the Victoria Embankment was the first area of London in which electric lights were installed in 1870, shortly after this stereograph was produced. These illuminations were the source of much interest among Londoners, who flocked to the riverside at nightfall to see them. The original lamp standards can still be seen along the river today, bearing Timothy Baker's distinctive design of entwined dolphins.

IN CONTRAST, THIS modern photograph was taken at around 4 a.m. on a summer's morning from Hungerford footbridge, which connects Charing Cross Station to the South Bank. At this hour the river is incredibly still, offering magnificent reflections of the London Eye on the South Bank and the Palace of Westminster opposite. County Hall can be seen behind the Eye, and Westminster Bridge is empty of traffic; the city looks peaceful in the moonlight. (Old image courtesy of the Library of Congress, LC-DIG-ppmsca-06824)

BRIDGE STREET, WESTMINSTER (BIG BEN)

THE CLOCK TOWER, which stands at the north corner of the Palace of Westminster, is probably the most iconic feature of London's skyline. The name Big Ben actually refers to the 14-ton bell that sounds the hour rather than the clock tower itself, though tourists and Londoners alike often overlook this fact. Cast in the Whitechapel Bell Foundry (which is still in operation today), Big Ben was named either after MP Sir Benjamin Hall who oversaw the installation of the bell, or contemporary boxing champion Benjamin Caunt. The tower itself stands at 106m high (320ft). Designed by Augustus Pugin, the clock is the largest of its kind in the world.

This photograph was taken in the late 1880s, not long after Big Ben's chimes sounded across London for the first time on 31 May 1859. This view facing up Bridge Street from Parliament Square shows a bustling scene of elegant horse-drawn carriages and omnibuses bearing top-hatted gentlemen towards Westminster Bridge.

Although the tower was, along with the rest of the Palace of Westminster, badly damaged during the Blitz, it continued its perfect time-keeping throughout the Second World War. However, as the building was such a distinctive landmark, the clock dials themselves were darkened at night to prevent guiding German pilots.

TODAY THE SCENE looks very similar, though, as this night-time photograph shows, the London Eye can be seen in the distance behind Big Ben's beautifully illuminated clock tower. The distinctive sound of Big Ben remains a quintessentially British sound, and these chimes are broadcast live every day on BBC radio.

WESTMINSTER ABBEY

WITH ALMOST 1,000 years of history, Westminster Abbey is England's largest and most important church. It is thought that an abbey was first founded around AD 620 on what was then known as Thorney Island beside the Thames, after a fisherman saw a vision of St Peter.

This remains unproven as no trace of the original buildings remain, though we do know that in AD 960 St Dunstan, the Bishop of London, brought the first Benedictine monks to make their home at Westminster. King Edward the Confessor went on to build a new abbey on the site, which was consecrated on 28 December 1065, a few days before his death. Since William the Conqueror in 1066, every British monarch has been crowned in the abbey. The most recent monarch to be crowned here was, of course, Queen Elizabeth II in 1953.

King Henry III began constructing the abbey we see today in 1245, which replaced Edward the Confessor's earlier building with a magnificent church in the very latest Gothic style. The abbey continued to take shape over subsequent centuries up until 1745, when Nicholas Hawksmoor added the distinctive pair of towers at the entrance.

Westminster Abbey served as both a place of worship and a monastery, and a tomb for Britain's last seventeen kings and queens. Over the years it has also become the final resting place of soldiers (including the Tomb of the Unknown Warrior), poets such as William Blake and Robert Burns, writers Charles Dickens, Rudyard Kipling and Jane Austen, scientists Sir Isaac Newton and Charles Darwin, priests, heroes and prime ministers.

This charming nineteenth-century stereograph shows the front view of the abbey as seen from Victoria Street. The road in front of the building is buzzing with pedestrians and traffic. The people are dwarfed by the sheer scale of the abbey. Ladies carry parasols, indicating that it was a sunny summer's day. Some kind of building work seems to be going on to the left-hand side of the building and a crowd of people surround the entrance to the abbey, which was as popular an attraction then as it is today.

THIS CONTEMPORARY
PHOTOGRAPH of Westminster
Abbey was taken after dark
and shows the spectacular
floodlit façade. Aside from slight
modifications to the entrance, the
building seems virtually identical
to the old photograph, despite
suffering damage from incendiary
bombs during the Blitz. Many of
the stained-glass windows were
destroyed, but have since been
restored to their former glory.
Today red London buses and black
cabs replace the carts and people
on horseback seen in the old
stereograph. Large trees now line
the street, adding some greenery,
and the area immediately outside
the abbey has been pedestrianised.

BUCKINGHAM PALACE

OVERLOOKING ST JAMES' PARK, Buckingham Palace has been the home of Britain's monarchy since 1837. The present building stands on the site of Buckingham House, a large townhouse built by the Duke of Buckingham in 1705. It was later purchased by King George III in the nineteenth century, and was extensively enlarged by architects John Nash and Edward Blore. However, King George died before work was completed and it did not become the official residence of a monarch until Queen Victoria took the throne.

The photograph on the right, taken around 1920, shows the palace much as it is today. To the right of the palace stands the golden statue of Queen Victoria looking regally down the Mall, while a few suited businessmen stride purposefully past on their way to work. The impressive 108m-long façade can be clearly seen. Inside, the palace contains a staggering 775 rooms, of which nineteen are state rooms, along with fifty-two bedrooms for the royal family and their guests, 188 staff bedrooms, ninety-two offices and seventy-eight bathrooms.

BUCKINGHAM PALACE IS today a major attraction for visitors to London, and crowds of sightseers gather at the gates from early morning onwards hoping for a glimpse of royalty or the changing of the guards. Buckingham Palace's state rooms, ballroom and private gardens are opened up to the public during August and September every year while the Queen is at Balmoral. The photograph on the left was taken from the edge of St James' Park, with the beautifully kept flowerbeds in the foreground. The royal standard is flying above the palace, signifying that the Queen is in residence. The palace's best-known feature can also be seen here – the balcony from which the royal family greet the crowds, most recently to celebrate the wedding of Prince William and Kate Middleton in April 2011.

MARBLE ARCH

OPPOSITE SPEAKERS' CORNER in Hyde Park you will find Marble Arch, one of London's best-known monuments. Today it is marooned on a road island marking the junction of Park Lane, Oxford Street and Edgware Road, but originally the arch was situated on the Mall and served as the main gateway to the newly built Buckingham Palace.

Marble Arch was built in 1828 by Regency architect John Nash, who also designed Regent Street and Trafalgar Square. Nash took his inspiration from the Triumphal Arch of Constantine in Rome, which he saw during his travels in Italy. It is clad in white marble from the Carrara quarry in Tuscany, where the stone for ancient Rome's Pantheon and Michelangelo's sculpture of David originated.

Legend has it that Marble Arch was relocated because it was not large enough to accommodate the Queen's royal stagecoach. However, in reality it was moved when Buckingham Palace was extended, and repositioned in 1851 at the entrance to Hyde Park where the Great Exhibition was taking place.

In this sepia photograph dating from around 1900, the arch is pictured in its new location though, in contrast to today, no traffic can be seen. Two policemen stand guard, and legend has it that the structure contained three small rooms used as surveillance rooms up until the 1950s, making the arch the smallest police station in the world. In this picture the gateways of the arch are closed off by iron gates, as at this time only members of the royal family and members of the Royal Horse Artillery were allowed to pass through the central arch.

TODAY MARBLE ARCH can only be reached by an unappealing pedestrian subway. Despite this, it manages to attract thousands of tourists each year. However, plans are afoot to relocate the arch a second time to a more serene home within Hyde Park, where it will be more easily accessible to the public.

To the north of the arch is a plaque in the paving stones, marking the location of London's infamous gallows, the Tyburn Tree. Here, from the twelfth century to 1783, an estimated 50,000 criminals and miscreants were publicly executed. The three-legged triangular design of the gallows allowed several people to be executed at once. Hangings were a popular spectator sport among Londoners, and thousands would come to watch, with many paying to view from specially built stands.

ROTTEN ROW, HYDE PARK

ROTTEN ROW IS the name given to a broad track that runs along the south side of London's Hyde Park. It leads from Hyde Park Corner (where Marble Arch is now located) to the Serpentine boating lake. During the eighteenth and nineteenth centuries, Rotten Row was a fashionable place for upper-class Londoners to be seen out for a stroll in their finery, or riding in their elegant horse-drawn carriages. Today Rotten Row is still maintained as a place to ride horses in the centre of London, but it is little used.

The space we now know as Hyde Park was originally Henry VIII's private hunting ground, stocked with deer and wild boar. However, in 1637 Charles I opened the park to the public for the first time. William III established Rotten Row at the end of the seventeenth century. Having moved his court to Kensington, William wanted a safer way to travel to his previous residence of St James' Palace.

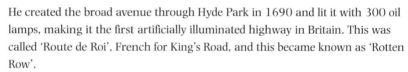

He created the broad avenue through Hyde Park in 1690 and lit it with 300 oil lamps, making it the first artificially illuminated highway in Britain. This was called 'Route de Roi', French for King's Road, and this became known as 'Rotten Row'.

This old photograph taken around 1900 shows Rotten Row and the South Carriage Drive near Marble Arch. Taken on a sunny summer's day, the trees are in leaf and the roadways are busy with people in carriages and riding horses. The pavements are lined with people out for a walk, with the gentlemen sporting bowler hats, black suits and walking canes while the ladies wear silk summer dresses and elegant bonnets. Some ladies can be seen riding side-saddle through the park.

TODAY'S VIEW OF Rotten Row is much the same, and the bridleway on the right remains unchanged. The sand-covered avenue is used by the Hyde Park Stables, who hire out horses to the public and offer riding lessons. It is also used by the Queen's Household Cavalry for exercising their horses. In this photograph, two riders can be seen in the background enjoying the sunshine. On the road, London taxi cabs replace the elegant carriages of a century ago, along with cyclists, joggers and pedestrians. Hyde Park is an oasis occupying 350 acres in the very heart of the city, making it one of the largest open spaces in London. It is one of the capital's oldest parks and features a boating lake, fountains, a meadow, cafés and over 4,000 trees. (Old image courtesy of the Library of Congress, LC-DIG-ppmsc-08575)

31

ROYAL ALBERT HALL

ROYAL ALBERT HALL in Kensington was the vision of Prince Albert, who wanted to dedicate a building in central London to art, music and science. A mosaic frieze of figures depicting 'The Triumph of Arts and Sciences' runs around the upper storeys. Shaped like a Roman amphitheatre, the hall was completed in 1871 by engineer Francis Fowke. Although the hall

looks circular, it is in fact elliptical in shape, and was originally designed to accommodate 8,000 people, though today's health and safety laws have put a maximum capacity of 5,500 for the venue. Unfortunately, when the hall was opened it became apparent that the acoustics inside were extremely poor. Due to the notorious echo, the hall was jokingly dubbed 'the only venue where a British composer could be sure to hear his work twice'. Various innovations were introduced to counter the problem, though it was not until 1969 that the issue was rectified thanks to the installation of unusual flying-saucer shaped fibreglass discs, designed to diffuse the echo.

In this stereograph, an elegant horse-drawn carriage waits at the bottom of the steps in front of Joseph Durham's statue of Prince Albert. Taken not long after the hall's completion, the building looks immaculate and new.

ROYAL ALBERT HALL is today one of the most famous venues in the world, not just for concerts but also for exhibitions, meetings, scientific debates and lectures, just as Prince Albert intended. Since the hall opened in 1871, it has seen concerts conducted by Wagner, Verdi, Elgar and Rachmaninov, followed more recently by musical legends Frank Sinatra, Jimi Hendrix, The Beatles, Oscar Peterson, The Who, The Rolling Stones and Led Zeppelin. The hall also hosts the world's largest classical music festival, The Proms, every year.

As seen in this modern photograph, the appearance of the Royal Albert Hall has altered very little, though a £20 million renovation plan to improve the auditorium's ventilation, seating and technical facilities has recently been completed inside. (Old image courtesy of the Library of Congress, LC-USZ62-133252)

ST PAUL'S CATHEDRAL
FROM BANKSIDE

THE SOUTHERN BANK of the river Thames offers the perfect view of St Paul's world-famous dome as it rises above the city from its perch on Ludgate Hill. This is the spot that Roman settlers supposedly chose to build a temple for their goddess Diana. Whether or not this is true, St Paul's is the fourth cathedral to occupy this site since AD 604. Viking raids, lightning bolts, and of course the Great Fire of London in 1666 destroyed the preceding Saxon and Norman cathedrals before Christopher Wren began work on the beautiful building we see today.

IN 1896, WHEN this photograph was taken, the riverbank in front of the cathedral was a busy jumble of buildings alive with industry and shipping traffic. London's river trade reached its peak in the eighteenth and nineteenth centuries, with wharves and warehouses lining both banks for miles along the Thames. Ships containing hundreds of thousands of tons of cargo travelled the waters of the Pool of London every year.

On the opposite bank of the river, architect Sir Giles Gilbert Scott (who was also responsible for Battersea Power Station and the famous red telephone box) built Bankside Power Station in 1952, which he intended to be a 'Cathedral of Power' reflecting neighbouring St Paul's.

TODAY THIS STRIKING red-brick building has been reinvented by architects Herzog & de Meuron, and is now the Tate Modern gallery. The stretch of river between Bankside and the City has also been transformed by the Millennium Bridge. This visually striking and complex structure was the result of a collaboration between architects Foster & Partners and British sculptor Sir Anthony Caro. The unique steel suspension bridge was opened in June 2000, the first new pedestrian bridge to be built over the Thames for 100 years. However, the bridge was closed shortly after its opening after it was found to 'wobble'. It reopened in 2002 after structural modifications, but is still popularly known among Londoners as 'The Wobbly Bridge'.

In its entirety, the bridge measures 325m in length with a 4m-wide aluminium walkway. The eight suspension cables are tensioned with a force of 2,000 tons against the piers set into each bank, which is enough to support 5,000 people walking over it simultaneously. The suspension cables are cleverly designed to dip at intervals, allowing completely uninterrupted views up and down the river.

The Millennium Bridge boasts what is possibly the best view of St Paul's Cathedral, especially at night when both the bridge and cathedral are floodlit to great effect. In this photograph you can see why the bridge is also known as the 'Blade of Light'.

ST PAUL'S CATHEDRAL

THIS BEAUTIFUL SEPIA photograph dating from around 1900 shows the elegant façade of St Paul's Cathedral. In the foreground a motorbus can be seen, and a few pedestrians mill about. The dome of the cathedral and the streets in the background are slightly obscured by a mist coming in from the river, or perhaps one of London's 'pea-souper' fogs. In the eighteenth and nineteenth centuries London became notorious for its thick yellow smog, which was said to give the air the consistency of pea and ham soup. This was the result of millions of chimneys billowing smoke into the atmosphere from burning coal. In fact, in this image you can see that, like many London buildings at this time, much of the stonework of the cathedral is blackened and dirty thanks to the smoky air.

This old photograph appears to have been taken from an elevated vantage point directly opposite the entrance to the cathedral. From this angle you can see the dome and the West Towers in their entirety. These towers never featured in Wren's original plan for the building; he added them in 1707. The right-hand tower has elegant 5m-diameter clock faces on three of its sides, though the left-hand tower simply has holes where the clocks would have been. Curiously, the roof of each tower sports a golden pineapple – a symbol of hospitality, peace, and prosperity.

IN THIS MODERN photograph taken on a bright summer's afternoon, St Paul's is viewed from street level. Tourists crowd the pavement and stairs in front of the cathedral and black cabs collect fares. In contrast to the old image, the Portland stone façade of the cathedral has now been restored to its original cream colour thanks to a £40 million, fifteen-year restoration project – the first time the building has been restored both inside and out since its completion in 1711. This was done to mark the cathedral's 300th anniversary on 21 June 2011, and, as a result, Christopher Wren's masterpiece looks as fresh and new as the day he completed it.

In this picture you can also see the triangular relief between the towers, depicting the conversion of the cathedral's patron saint to Christianity. Above it stands a statue of St Paul himself, flanked by other apostles and the four evangelists. This was the work of Francis Bird (between 1718 and 1721), who was greatly influenced by the church architecture of Rome. Bird also carved the statue of Queen Anne that stands in front of St Paul's. Anne was the reigning monarch at the time of the cathedral's completion.

St Paul's Cathedral is best known for its iconic dome, which since its construction has been one of the best-loved features of London's distinctive skyline. Measuring over 110m in height, it is one of the largest cathedral domes in the world and weighs an incredible 65,000 tons. The golden ball that crowns Wren's dome weighs 7 tons alone and has a diameter of 1.8m – room enough to contain ten people.

LONDON BRIDGE

FOR NEARLY 2,000 YEARS a bridge has spanned the river Thames at the same spot, linking
Southwark to the City. The first London Bridge was built around AD 52 by the invading Roman
Emperor Claudius. This was burned to the ground two years later by a vengeful Boudicca and
her army. Since then the bridge has been rebuilt and destroyed many times throughout London's
lively, and often violent, history. The well-known nursery rhyme 'London Bridge is Falling Down'
is believed to date back to around AD 1000, when the bridge was once again destroyed, this time
by invading Vikings. However, its best known incarnation was during medieval times. Engravings
from the 1600s show a bridge crowded with homes, shops and even a chapel – a city in itself –
supported upon nineteen stone and timber arches spanning the water. The southern end was
defended by a drawbridge and gatehouse, upon which the heads of unfortunates executed at the
Tower were displayed as both a curio and a warning to others.

The bridge was such a substantial structure that the stone arches which supported it restricted the flow of the Thames to the extent that in winter the river often froze over entirely, allowing London's famed Frost Fairs to take place. Many of the buildings covering the bridge were destroyed during the Great Fire of London in 1666, but, even so, the bridge itself survived for nearly 600 years before a new London Bridge was built slightly upstream in 1825, by engineer John Rennie. The old bridge remained until the new bridge was completed in 1831.

This atmospheric old photograph, taken around 1900, looks southwards across Rennie's London Bridge. Horse-drawn carts, omnibuses and pedestrians flow along the roadway as far as the eye can see. Around the time that this photograph was taken, it was estimated that the bridge was the busiest point in London, with 8,000 people crossing on foot and 900 crossing in vehicles every hour. London Bridge was widened between 1902 and 1904 from 16m to 20m, in an effort to combat London's increasingly problematic traffic congestion. In the background, behind the wharves and warehouses that line the river, the distinctive tower of Southwark Cathedral can be seen.

THE LONDON BRIDGE we know today opened on 17 March 1973. Designed by engineers Mott, Hay & Anderson, their brief was to engineer a bridge that was simple, functional and long-lived. The result looks virtually the same as its predecessor (which in 1970 was sold off to an American oil tycoon for £1 million and shipped to Arizona), though it is in fact much wider in order to cope with modern traffic. In this contemporary photograph, taken at rush hour from around the same spot as the old picture, commuters flood across the bridge on their way from their offices to London Bridge railway station, though double-decker buses have replaced carts and omnibuses. The warehouses lining the river have mostly been replaced with glass offices, and in the distance behind the cathedral you can see London's new skyscraper, Strata SE1, one of the first buildings in the world to incorporate wind turbines into its structure.

MONUMENT TO THE GREAT FIRE OF LONDON

BUILT TO COMMEMORATE one of the most famous moments of London's epic history, the Monument was designed by Sir Christopher Wren and Dr Robert Hooke. Completed in 1677 (twelve years after the fire began in a baker's house in Pudding Lane), this impressive column of Portland stone was intended to celebrate the new city which had emerged from the ashes. The fire started on Sunday 2 September and raged for four days and nights, swiftly engulfing the closely built medieval streets and thatched, timber-framed houses, aided by high winds. A firestorm took hold, and it is thought that temperatures reached up to 1,650 °C – hot enough to melt the huge chains and padlocks used to secure the city gates. Although most Londoners managed to escape the conflagration, it changed the landscape of the city forever, damaging 13,000 homes and 460 streets, as well as four city gates, eighty-seven churches and the old St Paul's Cathedral. Many residents were forced to relocate to the suburbs of the city – where they remained, easing overpopulation.

The Monument is 61m high, surmounted with a copper urn, giving the effect of a halo of flames. Inside the Doric column winds a spiral staircase. It stands in Monument Street off Fish Street Hill on the site of St Margaret's Church – the first to be destroyed by the blaze. The height of the column is also said to represent the distance between the Monument and the site in Pudding Lane where the fire originated.

IN THE OLD photograph dating from 1880, the Monument is viewed from Monument Street, with many horse-drawn traders' carts lined up in the foreground. The houses to the left have today been replaced by office buildings and the area of waste ground beside them has also been built upon. Few actual residential buildings remain in the City itself today. The Monument remains unchanged, though its location within London's Square Mile means that nowadays it is surrounded by unremarkable office buildings, fast-food outlets and coffee bars. Horses and carts have been replaced by delivery vans, scooters and motorbikes. In the new photograph, taken at dusk in late summer, office workers enjoy an after-work drink outside the bars surrounding the pedestrianised space at the foot of the Monument. The incredible views of the city from the top of the Monument still attract thousands of tourists each year. It is open daily between 9.30 a.m. and 5.30 p.m., and costs £3.

THE VIEW FROM
THE MONUMENT

THE 311 SPIRAL STEPS of Wren's colossal Monument to the Great Fire of London are climbed every year by over 150,000 visitors wishing to experience the awe-inspiring views of the city visible from the top. This old photograph shows the view looking westwards to St Paul's Cathedral. The wide thoroughfare of King William Street can be seen to the right of the picture. Immortalised in T.S. Eliot's poem 'The Waste Land', this street runs from the Bank of England through the heart of the financial district, meeting Poultry, Lombard Street and Threadneedle Street, and stretching southwards to London Bridge. Horse-drawn carts and omnibuses are the only traffic, and densely packed houses, pubs and office buildings (including the headquarters of the Aerated Bread Co., bottom right) jostle for space.

Today's panorama is very different. Where once a forest of church spires pointed heavenwards from seemingly every street corner, today there are strikingly few. The most

obvious of the survivors are the dome of St Paul's, and, in the centre of the photograph, the spire of St Mary-le-Bow with its famous Bow Bells, rebuilt by Wren after the Great Fire. Many of London's other churches were either destroyed during the Blitz, were subsequently demolished, or find themselves obscured by looming steel, concrete and glass office buildings. Today it is cranes that dominate the city's horizon rather than spires, as London's skyline continues to evolve.

However, this is not to say that London's modern skyline isn't full of interest. At the right of the photograph the wedding-cake style steeple of St Bride's Church in Fleet Street can be glimpsed, and to the left of St Paul's the 177m-high BT Tower can be seen in the distance over towards Regent's Park. Further to the right, Richard Rogers' innovative Lloyd's building, with its lift shafts, staircases and utility pipes on the outside, can be discerned beside the distinctive three towers of the 1960s Barbican buildings which dominate the skyline to the east.

TODAY THE OBSERVATION gallery is enclosed by wire mesh, added in 1842 to prevent suicides and accidental falls. Nonetheless, this doesn't detract from the dizzying 360° panoramic views of the city that the Monument offers. Many of London's iconic landmarks can be seen on a clear day from this unique vantage point, including Battersea Power Station, the Shard, the GLA, Tower Bridge, the Gherkin, the Tower of London and Canary Wharf.

THE ROYAL EXCHANGE

THE ROYAL EXCHANGE was founded in 1565 by the successful Elizabethan merchant Sir Thomas Gresham, as the City of London's centre of commerce. It is positioned at the busy intersection where Cornhill, Poultry and Threadneedle Street converge. As the old photograph from 1894 illustrates, the Royal Exchange stands at one of the busiest intersections in London and the street is a veritable chaos of horse-drawn hackney carriages, goods wagons and omnibuses. This junction was described by observers as one densely packed, slowly moving mass of traffic which pedestrians could only negotiate with difficulty. Before the days of traffic lights, it was the job of the City police force to create order out of traffic chaos, as seen in the bottom left-hand corner of this picture.

The original Royal Exchange building was designed around a central courtyard where traders could meet and trade surrounded by shops and offices. It was opened by Queen Elizabeth I on 23 January 1571. Like many other buildings in the city walls, it was destroyed during the Great Fire, and its next incarnation also burnt down in 1838. The Royal Exchange building seen today was designed by Sir William Tite and follows the same layout as the original.

The classical front façade consists of an elegant Corinthian portico supported by eight pillars reached by a broad flight of stairs. Inside is a central quadrangular courtyard. Here merchants would meet and trade, and shops and offices were housed in elegant colonnades lining the courtyard. This classical architecture provides a distinct contrast to Norman Foster's distinctive Gherkin skyscraper which peeks from behind the roof of the Exchange and stands a few streets to the east. In front of the building, the equestrian statue of the Duke of Wellington, designed by Chantrey in 1844, can be seen surrounded by railings. The unusual golden grasshopper weathervane which adorns the top of the building is a reference to the founder of the Exchange, as the grasshopper featured upon Gresham's family coat of arms.

TODAY THE ROYAL EXCHANGE is a luxury shopping centre attracting well-heeled City workers with designer labels such as Hermes and Prada, and jeweller's Tiffany & Co., alongside cafés and restaurants.

TOWER BRIDGE

LONDON'S TOWER BRIDGE is undoubtedly one of the most unusual and iconic bridges in the world. It came into existence because of the population explosion in the East End during the nineteenth century. At the time, London's bridges were all situated further to the west and an easterly bridge was desperately required for both vehicles and pedestrians. An ordinary bridge would disrupt the passage of tall-masted ships negotiating the waters in and out of the busy Pool of London so, in 1876, the City of London Corporation formed the Special Bridge or Subway Committee to find a solution to this problem. The winning design was a collaboration between engineer Sir John Wolfe Barry (son of Sir Charles Barry who designed the Houses of Parliament) and architect Sir Horace Jones. Their intelligent and original design was a cross between a

suspension bridge and a bascule bridge. When a ship needed to pass, the bridge's central roadway lifted using a steam-powered system of hydraulics. A high walkway between the two towers of the bridge allowed pedestrians to continue to cross the river when the bridge was open. The twin turrets were clad in stone and were designed to complement the neighbouring Tower of London.

As seen in this photograph, Tower Bridge opened to great fanfare on 7 July 1894. The river is crowded with steamboats decorated with bunting, barges and rowing boats crammed with people wearing their Sunday best. The bridge itself is packed with many hundreds of people who have come to marvel at Victorian London's latest feat of engineering. At the moment this picture was taken, the Trinity Yacht was passing through the open bridge.

OVER A CENTURY LATER, Tower Bridge itself has altered little in appearance. The colour of the ironwork has been changed many times over the years (originally brown) and today it is blue and white. Today, the bascules are still operated by hydraulic power, but since 1976 they have been driven by oil and electricity rather than steam. The high-level walkway has been closed since 1910 due to lack of use. It also had a reputation for attracting unsavoury characters such as pickpockets and prostitutes. Instead, the walkway has now been glassed in and houses the Tower Bridge Museum. The bridge is beautifully floodlit at night, as seen in this contemporary photograph. The promenades on either side of the river are popular with tourists and photographers, as many interesting London attractions are located in the vicinity, including Tower Bridge, HMS *Belfast* and City Hall.

VIEW OF
THE TOWER OF LONDON
FROM TOWER BRIDGE

TAKEN FROM THE pedestrian walkway at the top of the new Tower Bridge, this interesting photograph dating from around 1890 gives a unique view over the Tower of London. Covering 18 acres in total and enclosed by a double battlemented wall, this ancient fortress stands on the bank of the Thames to the east of the City, just outside the old city walls. The Tower was originally surrounded by a deep moat, but this was drained in 1843, a few decades before the picture was taken. In this image the grounds surrounding the Tower have been neatly landscaped, and the wide promenade by the river planted with trees.

Founded by William the Conqueror shortly after the Battle of Hastings in 1066, the original structure took the form of a wooden stronghold surrounded by a palisade and moat to guard against

invaders. This was replaced in 1077 by the much more impressive and permanent White Tower. At 27m (90ft) high it was the tallest building in London at the time, intended to overawe the local population and impress upon them the prowess of the conquering Normans. The White Tower was so called because its 12ft-thick walls, built from imported Caen stone, were originally whitewashed. In subsequent years, however, the walls were clad in Portland stone, and the scene in this photograph is very unlike how it would have appeared when the Tower was built. The other buildings were erected at different periods, in a jumble of differing architectural styles. During the Tower of London's lively history, it has been used as a royal refuge, the home of the Royal Mint from 1300, the Crown jewels and Royal Menagerie, as well as a notorious prison which earned a grim reputation as a site for executions from 1386 to 1747.

At the time this photograph was taken Tower Bridge itself was still under construction, and to the bottom right piles of stone are visible along with rickety scaffolding where the base of one of the towers is still underway. Down below on the Thames is a jumble of barges, sailing and rowing boats. The tide is out, allowing workmen to load or unload more timber for scaffolding onto the beach.

IT IS NOT possible to replicate this wonderful old scene precisely today because the Tower Bridge walkway has been glassed in, restricting the view. Nevertheless, in the contemporary photograph the ancient stones of the Tower provide an interesting contrast to the futuristic steel and glass skyscrapers and office buildings of the modern City, as London's financial district encompasses the Tower's walls. The Gherkin stands just to the left of William the Conqueror's White Tower, with the new Heron Tower (designed by architects Kohn Pedersen Fox) positioned in the centre of the photograph. Tower 42 is directly behind and the dome of St Paul's is to the far left. The Tower of London jetty can also be seen, where tourists can board boats for tours along the Thames.

VIEW FROM
TOWER BRIDGE

THIS SPECTACULAR PHOTOGRAPH of the city was taken from the walkway at the top of Tower Bridge during the early 1890s. From this unusual vantage point looking westwards up the river Thames you get a bird's-eye view of London. The river itself is alive with activity, and there are sailing boats and steamboats with barges and lighters moored to them. These vessels would have been used to unload cargoes from ships on the Thames during this time, when river trade was at its height and the Thames was the busiest port in the world. Wharves and warehouses line the southern bank of the river, where cargoes would have been stored. Upstream you can see London Bridge with Southwark Bridge beyond. The distinctive tower of Southwark Cathedral can be seen nearby on the left. Beyond the river, London's skyline bristles with the spires of countless churches as far as the eye can see.

Today, the walkway of Tower Bridge is glassed in to house a museum, but it is still just about possible to replicate this view by holding your camera out of the window. The southern bank of the Thames is dominated by London's newest skyscraper, the Shard of Glass. Designed by architect Renzo Piano, this building is clad entirely in glass, and its unique crystalline façade is designed to reflect the sky. At 310m (1,016ft) the Shard is the tallest building in western Europe, described by the architect as a 'vertical city' containing offices, restaurants, hotels and apartments, topped with London's highest public viewing

gallery. However, the decision to go ahead with this building has been contentious among Londoners who feel that the Shard's sheer size is out of keeping with the scale of the city's other buildings. Indeed, it can be seen from all over London, and dwarfs the dome of neighbouring St Paul's and the Tower of London, part of which can be seen here on the right-hand bank.

THE SAILING SHIPS on the Thames have nowadays been replaced by pleasure boats that operate tours along the river from Tower Pier. In the centre of the photograph is HMS *Belfast*, a Royal Navy cruiser launched in 1938 to fight German warships during the Second World War, and which played a key role in the Normandy Landings. Today HMS *Belfast* is permanently moored here and serves as a floating museum, showing what life was like on board ship during the war.

Offices have replaced the wharves and warehouses that once lined the river, and on the southern bank is a picturesque walkway lined with wine bars, pubs, shops and restaurants. This image also features the new London Bridge, built in 1973, which replaced the five stone arches of the older bridge completed in 1831. In the distance to the left of the picture you can see the London Eye and the distinctive chimney of the Tate Modern. On the right-hand bank of the Thames can be seen the dome of St Paul's Cathedral and the Monument.

THE TOWER OF LONDON

THIS SEPIA PHOTOGRAPH dating from 1890 shows the Tower of London as seen from across the Thames. Sailing boats and other vessels are moored in the foreground. Outside the entrance to the Tower, a group of people look out towards the southern shore of the Thames. Even then, the Tower was a very popular attraction and perhaps they had come to see the Crown jewels, a priceless symbol of the British monarchy.

The contemporary photograph of the Tower shows the scene at sunset in early autumn. The Tower complex looks virtually the same as it did in the late 1890s, though the trees are now mature and the elegant sailing ships have been replaced by a modern cruiser. In this case it is the *Dutch Master* which transports tourists up and down the Thames on sightseeing tours. The two outside decks are crowded with passengers as the boat heads for the Tower of London jetty to the left of the picture.

The walls of the Tower once enclosed the famous Royal Menagerie. It was traditional for kings and queens from different countries to send each other unusual animals as gifts, and it is thought that the Tower was home to a collection of exotic beasts for over 600 years. This royal zoo included lions, tigers, snakes, elephants and a polar bear which was allowed to fish for its supper in the Thames on the end of a stout chain. In the eighteenth century the exotic creatures were a popular tourist attraction and could be viewed in exchange for either a small admission fee, or the donation of a dog or cat to feed the more carnivorous animals of the collection. Today, sculptures of lions in the grounds of the Tower are the only reminder that the menagerie once occupied the site.

THE CROWN JEWELS are still on show, including the world's most famous diamonds and spectacular jewel-encrusted crowns, sceptres, swords and robes, which have been used in the coronation of England's kings and queens for centuries.

The Tower remains one of London's most fascinating destinations and offers a unique glimpse of the city's history. With its Crown jewels, ravens and beefeaters, today it attracts over 2 million visitors a year.

LOOKING EAST

THIS OLD PHOTOGRAPH dating from the late 1900s shows the easterly view from the top of the Monument to the Great Fire of London. Down below runs Monument Street, close to where it joins Lower Thames Street. The large buildings bordering the river are Old Billingsgate Fish Market, and the Custom House is visible towards the centre of the picture. The white church spire of St Margaret Pattens is on the far left. From this lofty vantage point you can also see the Tower of London in the distance, with Tower Bridge spanning the river Thames and hazy, rolling hills and countryside beyond. Many ships can be seen on the river, and on the southern bank stand the Victorian warehouses of Butlers Wharf.

TODAY'S VIEW SHOWS a similar warren of streets down below, though new landmarks have appeared on London's horizon. To the left stands the business district of Canary Wharf on the Isle of Dogs, with the distinctive pointed roof of one of the capital's tallest buildings, One Canada Square. Further right, beside Tower Bridge on the southern bank of the Thames, is City Hall, home to the Mayor of London and the London Assembly. This unusual building was designed by Foster & Partners, and has been nicknamed 'the glass egg' and 'the beehive' by Londoners.

In front of City Hall, the Second World War cruiser HMS *Belfast* is permanently moored and acts as a floating museum.

This part of London was decimated by German bombs during the Blitz, and many old buildings seen in the old view have since been replaced by less characterful glass and steel office buildings.

LONDON DOCKS

ONCE THE BUSIEST port in the world, London's docks have been at the heart of the city since Roman times. Before the construction of the docks, ships were moored along the riverbank, where they would often wait several days for barges and other small boats to come and transport their cargoes away. As London's river commerce grew, new docks were built to accommodate the traffic. London Docks and its close neighbour St Katharine Docks were constructed by engineer John Rennie in 1805 and covered 120 acres with room for over 300 large vessels. The huge warehouses (like the one seen in this picture on the right) were capable of storing an incredible 220,000 tons of goods, plus a maze of vaults with the capacity to contain up to 8 million gallons of wine.

This old photograph was taken around 1890, when the shipping industry was at its height and the dock employed over 3,000 workers a day. The scene shows a hive of activity, with a seagoing merchant ship moored against the quay while barrels and sacks are unloaded by dockworkers. It is possible that the boats in this image had recently returned from Africa, the Far East or the West Indies, where they collected exotic cargoes of rum, spices, tea, African ivory, indigo, perfume, casks of valuable wine and even live turtles with which to make turtle soup. In the background, other vessels are lined up waiting their turn. Some of the ships have been painted with white bands to imitate armed naval vessels. Captains hoped that this might deter pirates if they saw their ship from a distance.

However, the golden age of the sailing ship passed and the docks became too small and old-fashioned to accommodate the massive cargo ships and shipping containers of the twentieth century. London Docks and St Katharine Docks closed in 1969 and were left to decay for decades, until an intensive programme of urban renewal in east London sought to make use of these marvellous spaces.

THIS CONTEMPORARY IMAGE shows St Katharine Docks today, which, in contrast to the bustle of its busy industrial past, is now an oasis of tranquillity, despite being located close to the heart of the City. The old warehouses have been tastefully converted into wine bars, art galleries, boutiques, restaurants and luxury apartments, arranged around a marina where state-of-the-art yachts rub shoulders with 250-year-old barges. The secluded riverside location, along with its proximity to Tower Bridge and other attractions, makes the dock a popular destination for tourists and Londoners alike.

FLEET STREET

FLEET STREET DERIVES its name from the river Fleet, which runs underground from its source in Hampstead Heath to the Thames beneath Blackfriars Bridge. This famed London street has become synonymous with newspapers and journalism. Fleet Street's journey to becoming the centre of London's printing industry began in 1500, when writer William Caxton's assistant, Wynkyn de Worde, set up England's first printing press in nearby Shoe Lane. In 1702 the world's very first

newspaper, the *Daily Courant*, originated here, to be joined in later years by the *Observer*, the *Sun*, the *Daily Mail* and the now defunct *News of the World*.

This old photograph from the 1890s was taken looking eastwards from outside the pub Ye Olde Cheshire Cheese. The street is alive with traffic and is lined with shops, taverns and coffee houses. A man pushes a handcart along the busy thoroughfare, while two horses strain to pull an omnibus packed with many top-hatted gentlemen. In the distance sits St Paul's, and in front the spire of St Martin-within-Ludgate, which Wren designed to contrast with the dome of his great cathedral. The Ludgate Hill Viaduct bridges the road, carrying the London, Chatham & Dover Railway over Ludgate Circus.

TODAY THE RAILWAY has been put underground and the viaduct removed. Sandwich shops and fast-food outlets have replaced coffee houses, though Fleet Street still boasts several pubs. In this modern photograph the distinctive lantern-shaped sign of Ye Olde Cheshire Cheese is still visible to the far left, and despite the passing centuries the pub itself seems remarkably unchanged, with cosy snugs, open fires and sawdust on the floor. Since the exodus of the newspaper offices to Wapping and Docklands in the 1980s, Fleet Street has become more associated with law than journalism, thanks to the nearby Inns of Court and barristers' chambers located in the surrounding warren of alleyways and courtyards.

YE OLDE CHESHIRE CHEESE

'I've seen all of England,' she said. 'I've seen Westminster Abbey and the Houses of Parliament and His Majesty's Theatre and the Savoy and the Cheshire Cheese ...'

(*Piccadilly Jim,* P.G. Wodehouse)

TUCKED AWAY IN Wine Office Court and entered via a narrow passage off Fleet Street, Ye Olde Cheshire Cheese was the first public house in the area to reopen in the aftermath of the Great Fire. It is named after the most popular cheese among Londoners at the time. A pub has existed on this site since 1538, though the vaulted beer cellars are thought to date back to the thirteenth century, when a Carmelite monastery stood on the site.

In keeping with Fleet Street's literary tradition, this pub was the favourite haunt of famed diarist Samuel Pepys and, later, Dr Johnson, who wrote the first English Dictionary published in 1755. Mark Twain, Arthur Conan Doyle and Charles Dickens are also said to have propped up the bar of the Cheese at one time or another, and the pub is in fact alluded to in Dickens' novel *A Tale of Two Cities*.

This charming stereograph was taken in the passageway outside the Cheshire Cheese. Local characters have come out to pose, including a policeman and the pub's barman, standing with his hands on his hips in the doorway. A lady is framed in an upstairs window and a group of men peer out of the passageway. At this time, cameras and the new art of photography were the cause of great fascination, and everyone wanted to be featured in a photograph.

TO TURN OFF Fleet Street today into the dimness of Wine Office Court is to step back in time, and, as this contemporary photograph illustrates, the scene today is remarkably unchanged. Although Fleet Street and its surrounds have been much modernised since the ravages of the Blitz, this forgotten alleyway retains a Dickensian charm. The exterior of the Cheese is virtually unchanged, along with the houses opposite. Beside the distinctive cheese-shaped sign which marks the entrance to the bar, you can make out the hand-painted noticeboard which lists the fifteen monarchs who have ruled since the pub first opened its doors. A sandwich shop now occupies the small building on the far right, rather than the barber's shop pictured in the stereograph. The interior of the pub seems to have changed little, with numerous gloomy bars, cosy snugs, open fires in wintertime and sawdust on the floor. (Old image courtesy of the Library of Congress, LC-USZ62-113943)

STAPLE INN

STAPLE INN IN High Holborn is one of London's very last examples of an Elizabethan timber-framed building. It was built in 1545 to serve as the city's wool staple, and originally took the form of a covered market. Here wool was weighed and taxed, and the inn also acted as a meeting place for merchants. Lawyers were often needed to mediate in legal disputes and so Staple Inn became one of the nine Inns of Chancery, where young solicitors were trained in preparation for the Inns of Court. It stills serves as offices for barristers and solicitors today.

THE OLD PHOTOGRAPH, taken around 1890, shows the building shortly after restoration. The lower storeys house shops, which in this image are shuttered – probably as the picture was taken early in the morning, as is further indicated by the fact that the road is empty of traffic. The archway towards the left of the picture leads into a leafy courtyard garden. Staple Inn survived London's Great Fire but suffered extensive bomb damage from a German V-1 in 1944. However, today it has been lovingly restored once again, and the modern photograph shows the building much as it was over a century ago. An entrance to Chancery Lane tube station can be seen to the right, and at street level the building now houses a mobile phone shop and a tobacconist's, with offices on the higher storeys occupied by lawyers, surveyors and accountants. The lantern on top of the pedestal in the old photograph has today been replaced with the statue of a silver dragon bearing a shield emblazoned with the cross of St George.

Looking at this magnificent building, it is possible to imagine what the streets of Elizabethan London looked like. With its overhanging upper storeys, and elaborate black-and-white timber framework, Staple Inn is undoubtedly one of the most impressive buildings to survive the Great Fire.

TEMPLE CHURCH

TUCKED AWAY DOWN a narrow alleyway, among the Inns of Court, lies the fascinating 800-year-old Temple Church. The design of this unusual building was inspired by the circular Church of the Holy Sepulchre in Jerusalem, where Jesus is said to be interred.

Built by the Knights Templar in 1185, Temple Church is one of only four remaining circular churches in England today. The Knights Templar was an order of crusading monks founded to protect pilgrims on their way to and from Jerusalem in the twelfth century. At this time, many Christians were undertaking pilgrimages to the Holy Land, though the journey was fraught with danger, and despite travelling in large groups many were slaughtered upon the highway by bandits. The Templars received large donations in both land and money for

their services, and chose to make their headquarters here beside the Thames. They leased their properties to lawyers, and so the Inns of Court were founded and remain here to this day. The order became increasingly wealthy and powerful, not least by founding an early form of banking. However, when the fight for the Holy Land was lost, the Knights' popularity faded. The King of France (who was in debt to the Knights) and the Pope were intimidated by the power of the brotherhood and forced them to disband.

THE OLD PHOTOGRAPH, taken around 1880, shows the church's distinctive circular design topped by a pointed tiled roof, much like a castle turret with the bell tower to the left. Beyond the railing lies a tiny sunken graveyard, newly planted with trees. This photograph is slightly eerie as it shows no people, but it is possible that it was taken early in the morning.

Nowadays the church stands in a peaceful courtyard away from Fleet Street's traffic and noise, though it feels somewhat hemmed in and overshadowed by the surrounding buildings, mostly lawyers' chambers. The original viewpoint is now occupied by a modern office building and, as a result, it was not possible to replicate the old image. The church itself looks a little different today, as the circular tower lacks its pointed roof. This was destroyed by German bombs during the Blitz, though the building has since been sensitively restored.

Temple Church has seen a surge of interest since the publication of Dan Brown's blockbuster novel *The Da Vinci Code*, which featured many of the legends surrounding the mysterious brotherhood. Fans of the book have been found searching the church for secret signs and passageways which might conceal the Holy Grail.

THE OLD CURIOSITY SHOP

THERE IS MUCH debate over whether or not the Old Curiosity Shop in Holborn's Portsmouth Street inspired the Charles Dickens novel of the same name. Nevertheless, this peculiar and charming little timber-framed building certainly looks like it could have been home to orphan Little Nell.

In this photograph taken in the early 1890s, this shop houses nothing more curious than a stationer's and a waste-paper merchant. The window to the left is piled high with balls of string, bottles of ink, accounts ledgers, reams of paper, manuscripts and other items. Dating from 1567,

the Old Curiosity Shop survived both the Great Fire and the Blitz. Legend has it that the building began life as a dairy on an estate given by King Charles II to his mistress. Built from the wood of old sailing ships, the precariously overhanging upper storey of this carefully preserved building gives an idea of what London streets must have been like many centuries ago.

THE OLD CURIOSITY SHOP is today the oldest shop remaining in central London. Tucked away in a side street off Lincoln's Inn Fields, it is now a marvellously quirky shoe boutique selling beautiful handcrafted shoes made in a workshop in the cellars. The cobbles have now been covered over with tarmac, and huge brick office buildings tower over this tiny shop, which seems incongruous in these modern surroundings.

THE ROYAL
COURTS OF JUSTICE

SITUATED ON THE STRAND, near Temple Bar and the Inns of Court, are the Royal Courts of Justice. Opened by Queen Victoria in 1882, this sprawling Gothic building was designed by lawyer-turned-architect George Edmund Street. Street was best known for designing churches, and, possibly as a result of this, the courts have a cathedral-like air. This impressive building was commissioned shortly after the Houses of Parliament, when the Victorian enthusiasm for Gothic architecture was on the wane. Street spared no expense on detail, and the building boasts turrets and a beautiful rose window over the entranceway. The entrance itself is lavishly decorated with carvings of eminent lawyers and judges of the time, along with

biblical and historical figures, including Moses, Solomon and Alfred the Great, with Jesus depicted at the highest point of the porch roof. A cat and dog are sculpted over the Judge's Entranceway, symbolising fighting litigants.

The old photograph was taken around 1890 – less than a decade after the building's completion. The Strand is bustling with traffic in the form of horse-drawn omnibuses covered in advertisements for various products, much like London buses today. Men wearing smart black suits and top hats crowd the pavements outside the entranceway to the law courts. To the far right you can see the statue of a dragon that guards the border to the City from his plinth in the thoroughfare. The distinctive ornamental clock can be seen above, and in the distance you can see the awnings of the many shops, pubs and coffee houses which lined Fleet Street at this time.

TODAY THE ROYAL Courts of Justice are England's main court for civil cases such as divorce, libel and appeals. Criminal cases are nowadays heard at the Old Bailey, located half a mile to the east. Constructed from an impressive 35 million bricks, the building contains eighty-eight courtrooms that are open to the public for all cases except a few family law disputes. In the contemporary photograph, taken on a summer's day, the building looks virtually the same as it did over a century ago, though the street outside is frequently lined with cameramen, journalists and TV reporters when high-profile cases are being heard. The Strand is still one of London's busiest streets, as seen in this photograph, and the statue of the dragon still stands guard on his road island. Further along, Fleet Street is lined with shops, bars, bookshops specialising in law books, fast-food outlets and pubs, though many buildings have now been turned into offices.

71

THE STRAND

IN OLD ENGLISH, the word Strand, meaning 'shore' or 'riverbank', harks back to a time when the Thames was much wider than it is now, and this street skirted the river. In Saxon times this road lay at the heart of London, or 'Lundenwic', which was in AD 600 a busy trading town occupying an area stretching from Fleet Street to Whitehall, and from the Thames to Covent Garden. Since then, The Strand has acted as a main artery bearing traffic westwards to and from the City. It was unpaved up until the sixteenth century when it became gentrified, lined with the palaces and mansions of bishops, earls and royal courtiers. Many of the palaces had watergates, allowing access onto the river for ease of travel. In this old photograph of The Strand, taken around 1894, the pavements are brimming with well-heeled gentlemen wearing black suits and top hats. The Elizabethan mansions have long since disappeared, and the street is lined with shops, newspaper offices and theatres. On the right is a line of elegant gas lamps, and horse-drawn carts laden with people making their way to and from the City.

At the centre of the photograph is the church of St Mary-le-Strand, built in 1714 by architect James Gibbs. He took his inspiration from Rome's baroque churches, which he came across during his travels though Italy. The most striking feature is the unusual spire, layered like a wedding cake with lavish baroque ornamentation. This elegant church now occupies a road island, and the busy thoroughfares which surround it have long since swallowed its graveyard. It is one of two 'island churches' in London, the other being St Clement Danes further along The Strand, the spire of which can be seen in the background. Thanks to the churches' proximity to this busy thoroughfare, traffic noise has bothered parishioners at prayer since the 1800s.

TODAY THE SCENE is not hugely different, except red London buses and black cabs have taken the place of horses and carts. Many trees have been planted, giving this street some much-needed greenery, and the pavements are still packed with tourists making their way to Somerset House and the Courtauld Gallery located there. St Mary-le-Strand looks much the same, and is the official church of the Women's Royal Naval Service (the WRENS); it has a Book of Remembrance for members who have died in service.

COVENT GARDEN

MARKETS HAVE ALWAYS played a central role in London life, and Covent Garden Market in the West End is no exception. For centuries the site where Covent Garden now stands was used to grow food for the monks of Westminster Abbey – until the Dissolution of the Monasteries, when land owned by the Church was sold off. Convent Garden, as it was then known, was bought by the Earl of Bedford. In 1630 his descendants commissioned architect Inigo Jones to design England's first public and arcaded piazza, inspired by Italy's architecture, providing a dramatic contrast to the narrow, winding streets of the time.

In 1649 this fashionable square began to play host to a modest open-air fruit and vegetable market. After the Great Fire of 1666 destroyed many of London's larger market venues, the small market grew to take over almost the entire piazza. As a result, the residents of the grand houses surrounding the square left to find more peaceful residences. Taverns, theatres and coffee houses opened up, and the area became popular with artists and writers – along with pickpockets and prostitutes.

In this fascinating old photograph, taken around 1890, the piazza is a chaos of wooden carts, crates, barrels and baskets containing every kind of fruit and vegetable imaginable. Londoners would flock here in their thousands to purchase fresh flowers and herbs, potatoes, strawberries, pears and more exotic treats such as coconuts and oranges. In the picture, market traders unload rickety horse-drawn wagons full of cabbages and turnips, and young boys wearing flat caps carry baskets. Gas lamps are dotted around because the

market opened at first light, with traders and buyers travelling the streets throughout the night. In the background you can see the neo-classical style building built in 1830 by architect Charles Fowler to enclose the market. In this image, the market workers are probably unloading goods and taking them into the undercover stalls inside.

DUE TO TRAFFIC congestion, in 1960 the market was relocated to the southern bank of the Thames, not far from Vauxhall, and the central building was redeveloped to become a shopping centre. Covent Garden is today one of London's most popular tourist attractions, with shops, boutiques, cafés, bars and restaurants, along with a small craft market selling souvenirs. There are also many theatres nearby, and the Royal Opera House occupies one side of the square. Covent Garden has always been famous for its many street performers and musicians, and Samuel Pepys described one of the earliest performances of a Punch and Judy puppet show here back in 1662. In this contemporary photograph, an acrobat entertains the crowds on a sunny afternoon. You can see that the old Georgian building, which formed the market, has been much altered and added to over the years.

SEVEN DIALS

SEVEN DIALS IN Covent Garden is so called because it is the crossroads
where seven roads converge. This interesting old photograph shows
Seven Dials as it was in the late 1800s. The Crown public house stands
on the corner decorated with enamelled signs boasting 'Courage Bitter,
Port, Stout and Ales', with another pub to the right. In fact, at one time
there was a pub on every corner of the Seven Dials junction. Outside in
the street a variety of curious London characters stare into the camera,
including two bearded gentlemen dressed like sea captains holding a
wheel, and a man wearing a hat standing with what appears to be a
sheep.

Earlham Street bears off to the right, where you can see a street
seller's barrow of vegetables; a wagon full of milk churns heads off
into the distance. To the left is Monmouth Street, lined with houses
and shops, with horse-drawn vehicles making their way towards
Shaftesbury Avenue.

Once a notorious slum, this photograph was taken before the area
became more gentrified, and poverty and squalor were still rife in

the surrounding courts and lanes of the rookery of St Giles, as this area was then known. In the seventeenth century, a pillar with six sundials stood at the centre of this junction, with the seventh dial formed by the shadow cast by the Monument itself. However, this landmark had been removed by the time this photograph was taken, as the Seven Dials had become a meeting place for thieves and other unsavoury local characters.

TODAY THE ARCHITECTURE of the Seven Dials has altered very little, and the Crown pub still stands on the corner looking remarkably similar to how it did over a century ago. However, today's Covent Garden is quite a contrast to the slum of the 1900s. In this picture you can see the replica of the original Seven Dials monument that was erected in the late 1980s.

THE BRITISH MUSEUM

ESTABLISHED IN 1753 to house the collection of artefacts belonging to physician Sir Hans Sloane, the British Museum is the oldest public museum in the world.

Sloane, a naturalist and collector, had accumulated around 71,000 objects over his lifetime, including antiquities from Greece, Rome, Egypt and the East; manuscripts; books; and prints by artists such as Albrecht Durer. He owned an extensive collection of natural specimens which were later moved to Kensington to form the basis of the Natural History Museum's collection. Not wishing for the collection to be broken up after his death, Sloane bequeathed his cabinet of curiosities to King George II in 1753.

The collection was housed in the seventeenth-century mansion Montagu House, situated in a small street in Bloomsbury. This building was extended over the years by architect Sir Robert Smirke to accommodate the ever-growing collection. Extra wings and floors were added around a central courtyard. It was here that Sir Robert's brother Sidney designed and built the famous domed reading room which housed the British Library. Here scholars came to view famous texts such as the Lindisfarne Gospels and the only surviving copy of Beowulf.

This old photograph dating from the late nineteenth century shows the imposing façade which forms the entrance of the museum, with its Ionic colonnade and Grecian-style portico. The building looks much as it does today, though gas lamps can be seen in the street and courtyard. Hardly any people can be seen, aside from a lone woman dressed in black pushing a baby in a huge perambulator up the street. The gates to the museum are closed, suggesting that this photograph was taken early in the morning or on a Sunday.

The museum was open to the public most days of the year, with the exception of a few periods of disruption during the First and Second World Wars when objects were put into storage to protect them from German bombs.

BY COMPARISON, THE modern photograph of the museum shows the courtyard alive with people. It is a popular meeting place for students and tourists, or office workers with packed lunches who visit the collections in their lunch hour. The façade itself looks virtually identical, though the central courtyard was extensively redesigned in 1998 by architect Norman Foster. His spectacular glass roof constructed from 1,656 individually shaped panes of glass created a covered square at the centre of the museum that today houses exhibition spaces and a restaurant.

Since opening its doors for the first time, the museum has granted free access to 'all studious and curious persons' and does so to this day. In the eighteenth century it received 5,000 visitors a year, and today this number stands at an impressive 6 million. Over the years, further interesting acquisitions were made, including the Rosetta Stone in 1802 and the Elgin Marbles from the Parthenon in 1816. There were also displays of exotic finds brought back from the South Sea voyages of Captain Cook and other explorers. Today the museum is home to the Ludlow man, Egyptian mummies and the Sutton Hoo hoard, among other treasures. (Old image courtesy of the Library of Congress, LC-DIG-ppmsc-08563)

OXFORD CIRCUS

IN THIS STEREOGRAPH dating from 1908, a smartly dressed couple are being driven in a very elegant coach drawn by immaculately groomed horses across Oxford Circus in London's busy West End. They are probably heading from the fashionable shops in Regent Street. The buildings in the background look smart and many have awnings to protect their goods from sunlight. The pavements are crowded with people.

Oxford Street follows the route of an old Roman road linking Hampshire with Colchester, and became one of the major routes in and out of the city. Up until the late 1700s it was known as Tyburn Road after the river Tyburn that ran just to the south of it, and which today flows beneath it. This street gained notoriety as the route taken by prisoners on their final journey from Newgate Prison to the gallows at Tyburn near Marble Arch. In the late eighteenth century, the Earl of Oxford purchased many of the surrounding fields and the area was developed. By about 1729, the road had become known as Oxford Street. During the nineteenth century the area was redeveloped by architect John Nash, along with nearby Regent Street, and became the fashionable district it is today.

TODAY OXFORD STREET is said to be Europe's busiest shopping street, boasting over a mile and a half of shops, including department stores such as John Lewis (opened in 1864) and Selfridges (opened in 1909). In this contemporary photograph, the scene remains remarkably similar, with the buildings in the background unchanged. To the left, Nike World occupies the elegant building decorated with Greek-style columns, and in the foreground red London buses and black cabs head to and from Shaftesbury Avenue and Charing Cross Road. Oxford Circus, London's second busiest underground station after Victoria station, is just out of shot to the right. In this photograph you can see the road markings of the newly installed 'diagonal junction' that allows shoppers to cross the intersection diagonally as well as at right angles. This Japanese innovation was originally invented to relieve pedestrian congestion in Tokyo, and London's Mayor, Boris Johnson, is hoping it will achieve the same result in the capital. (Old image courtesy of the Library of Congress, LC-USZ62-133249)

PALACE THEATRE

THIS OLD PHOTOGRAPH shows the Palace Theatre at
Cambridge Circus, the corner where Shaftesbury Avenue
and Charing Cross Road converge in London's busy West
End. The theatre originally opened in 1891 as the Royal
English Opera House, but within a year it had become
a music hall and was rechristened the Palace Theatre
of Varieties. In this scene the theatre must be newly
completed, and placards on the street outside show pictures
of the shows and star performers. Shaftesbury Avenue is
busy with traffic and pedestrians, and an elegant carriage
waits at the entrance.

No expense was spared in the building of this theatre,
and this photograph shows the distinctive terracotta and
Ellistown brick façade designed by Thomas Edward Collcutt.
The interior was no less opulent, decorated with green
Italian marble and gold leaf, and illuminated with over
2,000 electric lights at a time when many theatres were still
lit with gas lamps.

TODAY THE PALACE THEATRE is no less regal in its appearance and looks much as it did when it was built. The theatre is owned by renowned musical director Andrew Lloyd Webber and still puts on hugely popular shows. In recent years the musicals *Les Misérables*, *Jesus Christ Superstar* and *Whistle Down the Wind* have been staged here. In the contemporary picture you can see that the façade has been decorated with a huge glittered stiletto advertising the musical *Priscilla, Queen of the Desert*. Its perfect location on the edge of Soho, Covent Garden and China Town makes the Palace Theatre a popular destination.

REGENT STREET

NAMED AFTER THE Prince Regent
(later to become King George IV),
London's regal Regent Street
was constructed between 1811
and 1825. It was the vision of
innovative architect John Nash,
who wanted to bring more public
spaces and broader thoroughfares
to the city. Curved like a Roman
amphitheatre, this elegant street
was designed to connect Regent's
Park to the fashionable area of
Charing Cross, bypassing the
less salubrious Soho. Stretching
for almost a mile, Regent Street
extends from Waterloo Place near
Pall Mall through Oxford Circus
to Portland Place. It housed the
finest of London's shops, and in
this photograph taken around
1895 the street is thronged with
elegant horse-drawn carriages and
omnibuses, with well-dressed ladies
admiring the window displays.
Awnings protect the goods from
sunlight and the ladies carry
parasols, suggesting it is a bright
summer's day. A cart piled high
with boxes is delivering goods and
a boy wearing a sandwich board
advertises wares.

TODAY'S REGENT STREET looks not dissimilar to the old photograph, with its curved façades and designer shops. However, on closer inspection the architecture itself is quite different, particularly on the right-hand side of the street. This is because between 1895 and 1927 the street was completely redeveloped, and south of Oxford Circus none of John Nash's original buildings survive, although the street still follows his original layout. The new buildings are much more ornate than those originally created by Nash. However, they are still listed Grade II or above and form part of the Regent Street Conservation Area.

The Edwardians' enthusiasm for the newly invented department store meant that Nash's buildings were deemed old-fashioned and unsuitable, and Regent Street's small shops and narrow display windows were restricting trade. The modernised retail spaces attracted companies such as Dickins & Jones, Liberty & Co., and Hamleys toy shop, some of which remain to this day. Although several architects undertook the project, the new buildings shared a unified façade crafted from Portland stone and decorated with balconies, pillars and cornices to impressive effect.

Regent Street is still one of the major shopping streets in the West End. In this contemporary photograph, taken after dark, the street is busy with red London buses, tourists and shoppers drawn by the many famous fashion boutiques and department stores, such as the flagship Apple computer store, Aquascutum, and Jaeger, and the food quarter in nearby Heddon Street. Food and music festivals also draw visitors, cultural events are held here throughout the year, and the street is famed for its annual Christmas illuminations.

PICCADILLY
CIRCUS

THIS FAMOUS STREET in the heart of London's busy West End takes its name from Elizabethan tailor Robert Baker, who specialised in making fashionable collars known as 'piccadills'. He named his nearby home Pickadilly Hall, and so the street derived its name.

Piccadilly Circus is possibly best known for its fountain topped with a statue of an angel. The 'Angel of Christian Charity', designed by Sir Alfred Gilbert, was unveiled in 1893 and was the first ever sculpture to be cast from aluminium. It was created as a tribute to the good deeds of Victorian philanthropist the 7th Earl of Shaftesbury. However, with his bow and arrow and bare chest, Londoners quickly rechristened this figure Eros, a symbol of desire.

The old photograph taken in the early 1900s shows the winged statue in his original location in the centre of the circus. In this vibrant scene, people and cars surround the fountain, with many horse-drawn carts outside the theatres and shops. In the 1980s

the layout of Piccadilly Circus was redesigned and Eros was moved to his present home in the south-western corner, near Lillywhites sports shop. In the background, the popular variety theatre the London Pavilion (now the Trocadero) can be seen on the left, with the Criterion Theatre on the right.

IN THE HEART of London's West End, Piccadilly Circus still retains its energetic atmosphere, attracting many tourists and theatregoers, and provides a meeting place for those heading out for an evening on the town in nearby Soho. This street is so busy that there is the somewhat dubious saying that if you stand there long enough, you will encounter every person you know. Even late in the evening, when this contemporary photograph was taken, the fountain is surrounded by tourists. The buildings surrounding Piccadilly Circus are colourful, with neon lights and several large advertising hoardings covering the sides of the buildings facing onto the junction. These first appeared in 1910 with a large Bovril sign. Today the signs are somewhat more sophisticated, with moving images and LEDs advertising popular brands such as Coca-Cola and Samsung.

TRAFALGAR SQUARE

TRAFALGAR SQUARE WAS built to commemorate Britain's greatest naval victory – the Battle of Trafalgar in 1805. Designed by John Nash, it was intended as a space for public gatherings, meetings, celebrations and rallies. From the fourteenth to the seventeenth century, this site was occupied by the courtyard and stables of Whitehall Palace.

The square is presided over by the statue of Admiral Horatio Nelson, the nation's most famous sea lord, who died heroically at the Battle of Trafalgar. The 56m (184ft) granite column upon which he stands is the main focal point of the square. The sense of scale of this monument is deceptive, and the statue of Nelson stands at 5.5m, facing south-west towards his fleet at

Portsmouth. Legend has it that on the column's completion, fourteen stonemasons had a dinner party upon the top, complete with dining table and chairs, before Nelson's statue was put in place.

This beautiful sepia photograph was taken from the church spire of St Martin-in-the-Fields, with the equestrian statue of George IV visible in the foreground. In contrast to today, the square itself is virtually empty of sightseers, though it is completely surrounded by the bustle of traffic, old-fashioned double-decker buses, bicycles and cars

TODAY, THE TOWER of St Martin's is not open to the public, and instead this view was taken from the balcony of the National Gallery on the north side of the square. Trafalgar Square has been much modernised, with the addition of a café and other facilities, and the road in front of the gallery has now been pedestrianised so that it is no longer isolated on a road island. It is a major attraction for tourists and foreign students, who come to take photographs, visit the gallery and café, and climb upon the statues of lions at the foot of Nelson's Column.

Trafalgar Square still plays a key role in the life of the city, for public demonstrations, New Year's Eve revelry, and most recently celebrating the success of London's Olympic bid. In the run up to London 2012, a digital clock displayed the countdown of days, hours and minutes. The square is illuminated after dark by new state-of-the-art LED lighting and water-jets were installed in preparation for the Olympics.

THE NATIONAL GALLERY

SITUATED ON TRAFALGAR Square, the National Gallery is home to 2,300 paintings, including some of the best-known works of art in the world. It was founded in 1824 when Parliament purchased the picture collection of the banker John Julius Angerstein. These thirty-eight paintings formed the core of a new national collection, and in 1838 the National Gallery opened to the public.

This photograph, dating from around 1890, shows the impressive 450ft-long façade built in a Greek revival style by architect William Wilkins. Horse-drawn carriages pass on the road outside, and a group of schoolchildren bearing sketchbooks can be seen to the left. To the right stands the church of St Martin-in-the-Fields. A church has stood on this site since the thirteenth century; the current church dates to 1726 and was designed by architect James Gibbs. It became the final resting place of British painters William Hogarth and Joshua Reynolds.

TODAY'S VIEW Of the National Gallery has changed very little. The lack of traffic outside is really the only difference: Trafalgar Square was partially pedestrianised in 2003 to make it easier for visitors to reach the gallery. With its excellent location the gallery draws tens of thousands of visitors each year, all wishing to see world-famous works of art, including *The Rokeby Venus* by Velazquez, *The Hay Wain* by John Constable and works by Vermeer, Leonardo da Vinci and Vincent Van Gogh. The gallery is open 361 days of the year, and access is free.

St Martin-in-the-Fields now houses a soup kitchen for the homeless, as well as a café in the crypt.

ROYAL BOTANIC GARDENS, KEW

LOCATED IN SOUTH-WEST London between the villages of Richmond and Kew, the Royal Botanic Gardens were founded in 1759. The royal family spent their summers at Kew Palace, positioned near the Thames within easy sailing distance of London, and royal gardens were created nearby. Later, under the patronage of Queen Victoria, the ornate Victorian glasshouses were built to house the ever-expanding collection of exotic plant species brought back from voyages to the colonies. In 1840 the gardens were opened to the public, and the new railway links from Kew to London allowed visitors to flock to the gardens, which became a popular visitor attraction.

This photograph, dating from 1889, shows the interior of Kew's famous Waterlily House. Now a listed building, this greenhouse was built in 1852. At the time, it was the widest greenhouse in the world, specifically designed to house an 11m-wide circular pool to accommodate the gardens' collection of giant Amazonian water lilies, *Victoria amazonica*, named after Queen Victoria. As can be seen in this picture, these incredible aquatic plants can produce leaves which measure up to 2.5m across, and can support a person weighing up to 45kg.

TODAY THE INTERIOR of the Waterlily House looks much the same as it did in the 1890s, and still proves a popular tourist attraction. Orchids and other rare exotic plants hang from the ornate ironwork ceiling, while palms, ferns and tropical plants border the circular pool.

Kew's stunning glasshouses, including the Temperate House, the Waterlily House and the curvaceous Palm House, were built by engineer Richard Turner and designed by architect Decimus Burton (who also created Hyde Park Corner's Triumphal Arch). They are the largest and most important surviving Victorian glasshouses in the world. These incredible feats of architecture employed new shipbuilding technology which, in the case of the Palm House, allowed them to span large spaces using wrought iron and glass without the need for supporting columns. The result was an incredible building reminiscent of an upturned ship, with plenty of uninterrupted space in which huge palm trees could grow.

In 2003 Kew Gardens was awarded UNESCO World Heritage status, and today attracts around 2 million visitors annually. Set in 300 acres of beautiful gardens with six magnificent greenhouses, Kew boasts the world's largest collection of plant specimens. The grounds also feature a Chinese pagoda, a seed bank, Kew Palace, a museum and a treetop walkway.

If you enjoyed this book, you may also be interested in …

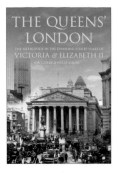

The Queens' London
JON CURRY & HUGO SIMMS

In 1897, *The Queen's London* was published. The work, a collection of some of the finest photographs of the capital ever taken, was produced to commemorate the Diamond Jubilee of Queen Victoria. In 2012, *The Queens' London* brings this story up to date. Pairing the beautifully captured vintage views with 180 images taken from identical vantage points in the London of Queen Elizabeth II's Diamond Jubilee, this book gives the reader a fascinating perspective on the history behind London's familiar streets.

978 0 7524 7011 5

A 1960s East End Childhood
SIMON WEBB

Do you remember playing in streets free of traffic? Dancing to The Beatles? Watching a man land on the moon? If the answer is yes, then chances are you were a child in the 1960s. This delightful compendium of memories will appeal to all who grew up in the East End during the Swinging Sixties. With chapters on games and hobbies, school and holidays, this wonderful volume is sure to jog memories for all who remember this exciting decade.

978 0 7524 7484 7

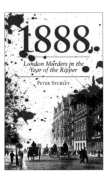

1888: London Murders in the Year of the Ripper
PETER STUBLEY

In 1888 Jack the Ripper made the headlines with a series of horrific murders that remain unsolved. But most killers are not shadowy figures stalking the streets; many are ordinary citizens driven to the ultimate crime by circumstance, a fit of anger or a desire for revenge. This book examines all the known murders in London in 1888. Why did a husband batter his wife to death after she failed to get him a cup of tea? How many died under the wheels of a horse-driven cab? Just how dangerous was London?

978 0 7524 6543 2

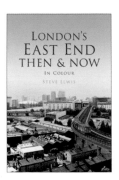

London's East End Then & Now
STEVE LEWIS

London's East End Then & Now is a superb collection of photographs showing scenes of yesteryear contrasted with modern colour views. The photographs and informative captions reveal the sometimes drastic changes which have taken place in the name of progress, not least to accommodate the 2012 Olympic Games. Drawing on detailed local knowledge of the community, and illustrated with a wealth of fascinating images, this book recalls what has changed in terms of buildings, traditions and ways of life.

978 0 7524 6430 5

Visit our website and discover thousands of other History Press books.

www.thehistorypress.co.uk